Creating Wealth from the Inside Out Workbook

Creating Wealth from the Inside Out Workbook

A step-by-step guide for changing how you think and feel about money

BY KATHLEEN BURNS KINGSBURY

Contents

Introduction 1

Chapter 1:   Creating Wealth from the Inside Out 5

Chapter 2:   Accept Your Money History 10

Chapter 3:   Your Money Mindset 21

Chapter 4:   Believe in Your Worth 35

Chapter 5:   Shift Your Money Mindset 42

Chapter 6:   Are You Ready to Change? 52

Chapter 7:   Create Opportunities to Receive Wealth 66

Chapter 8:   Financial Conversations 71

Chapter 9:   Your Financial Dream Team 83

Chapter 10: Practice, Not Perfection 92

Final Thoughts 98

Appendix I: A Wealth of Resources 99

Appendix II: Wealth Coaching Exercises 102

Acknowledgements 103

About the Author 104

Wealth is the ability to fully experience life.

Thoreau

Introduction

Do you ever feel anxious, scared, fearful, angry, or uneasy about money and wealth? Do you make resolutions to be more fiscally responsible only to end up maxing out your credit cards? Do you read books on personal finance, but never make time to implement the author's strategies? Or do you ignore money in your life hoping that it will take care of itself? If you answered yes to any of these questions, then this workbook and the *Creating Wealth from the Inside Out Program* is for you.

Creating Wealth from the Inside Out is a program developed to teach you easy, practical tools and techniques for examining and changing your money mindset to support a wealthier and richer life. When I released the *Creating Wealth From The Inside Out Audio Program* (available through my website at www.kbkwealthconnection.com) in April 2010, I received a great response from listeners who loved the program and requested more case studies, more tools, and more coaching exercises to help them understand and shift money mindsets. I created this workbook to respond to that request. It is designed to help you delve deeper into your money psyche.

You may use this workbook in conjunction with the audio program or as a stand-alone resource. To get the most impact, I highly recommend you utilize both resources in your quest to transform your money mindset. The workbook reinforces key concepts introduced in the audio program and provides a space for you to work out your thoughts in writing, a great next step for applying the lessons to your particular life circumstances.

As with all personal growth, taking action is the key to making change. This workbook and the coaching exercises in each chapter will help you do just that -- take action toward a healthier, more financially conscious you.

The *Creating Wealth from the Inside Out Workbook* takes you through a process of change that is highly effective. The work begins with coaching exercises geared toward gaining insight into your money history. You will then examine how your financial history impacts your current spending, saving, investing, and giving habits. You will also identify key areas for change and growth. Next, simple and effective tools are offered for letting go of money beliefs and attitudes that negatively impact your wealth. A practical solution for shifting these money messages is presented. Finally, guidelines for conducting productive financial conversations as well as tips for finding and interviewing qualified financial professionals are shared.

How to Use This Workbook

The program is most effective if you start at the beginning of the workbook and complete each chapter's wealth coaching exercise before moving to the next chapter. However, if you prefer to skip around the workbook and complete the exercises that resonate with you first, please feel free to do so. We each have unique learning styles and you know what works best for you.

Each coaching exercises is broken down into four sections – **Purpose, Getting Started, Activity,** and **Action & Accountability.**

- **Purpose:** This section gives a short explanation of the purpose of the coaching exercise.

- **Getting Started:** This section tells you the approximate time to allot to complete the exercise and what supplies, if any, are needed.

- **Activity**: This section is the meat and potatoes of the wealth coaching process. Each activity is carefully crafted to assist you in uncovering and discovering new insights into your thoughts, feelings, and habits around money.

- **Action & Accountability**: The key to transformation is committing to change by taking action steps. It is vital that you integrate your new insights and awareness into your life as soon as possible. Therefore, each coaching exercise ends with three steps: determining an action step, constructing a time frame for completing this action, and reaching out to connect with an accountability partner. An accountability partner is a trusted person, perhaps a friend who is also on the path to making positive change in their lives or a coach, who you select to support you in taking action. This person can be the same person or different people for each exercise. Often a wealth coach or a financial advisor can make a great accountability partner as he or she is objective, professionally trained, and not emotionally involved in your progress.

The Importance of Support

Changing your relationship with money takes time, patience, and support. It is important that you pace yourself as you complete the wealth coaching exercises in the workbook. Money is an emotional topic and difficult feelings may get stirred up. This is normal and part of the process of wealth coaching. In time these feelings will subside; however, if overwhelming feelings become too disruptive, please enlist some support from a financial therapist, wealth coach, financial advisor, or mental health professional. Asking for support is a sign of strength, can really enrich the wealth coaching experience, and often results in long-lasting behavioral change around money. Consult the list of resources in Appendix I: A Wealth of Resources, should you decide to get support.

My money coaching philosophy is based on my twenty years of experience as a behavioral change specialist in the field of psychology and my financial industry education and background. Over the past several years, I have coached, counseled, and spoken to thousands of men and women about mastering their money mindsets. I've been proud to witness countless personal and professional transformations. While I am an expert in the field of wealth psychology, I am not immune to financial challenges. I have weathered financial storms and used many of these coaching tools to work through difficulties of my own. As someone who has not only created this program, but practiced it, I am confident that you can also create true wealth in your life – if you start the work from the inside out.

Best wishes as you start your journey toward true wealth.

kbk
Kathleen Burns Kingsbury, LMHC, CPCC
Wealth Psychology Expert
Principal, KBK Wealth Connection

Chapter 1:   Creating Wealth from the Inside Out

Changing your thoughts, feelings, and behaviors around money and wealth is the key to improving your financial life and your ability to create a wealthy and fulfilling future. The process involves both psychological and behavioral components and can produce powerful, life-changing results.   While the concepts underlying human behavior and the psychology of change are complex, I created a simplified, three step formula for transforming your relationship with money. I call this method the **ABC's** of *Creating Wealth from the Inside Out*. **ABC** stands for **Accept, Believe,** and **Create.**

I firmly believe that if you *accept* and learn from your money history, *believe* in your ability to change unhealthy financial behaviors and attitudes, and *create* opportunities to practice receiving from others, you will not only master your money mindset, but also feel more peaceful and confident around money and finances.

The Meaning of Wealth

What does wealth mean to you? Does wealth mean having assets valued at a million dollars or earning a high six figure income or having enough money in the bank to live comfortably? Is it watching your kids grow up and get married, traveling the world, or working hard so you can leave your loved ones a sizable inheritance?

According to the Merriam-Webster Dictionary, wealth means an abundance of valuable material possessions or resources. Interestingly enough, the word originated in Middle English in the 13th century and comes from the word "weal," which is defined as a sound, healthy, and prosperous state of well-being. Historically, the word "wealth" includes both emotional and financial terms.

My personal definition of wealth is having enough financial and emotional assets so that you're not burdened with worries about money. You can breathe easy and enjoy life to the fullest when money doesn't weigh heavy on your mind. Your personal definition of wealth may vary from mine. That is okay! The amount of financial and non-financial resources it requires for you feel wealthy may differ from your partner, your children, your family, or your friends. Or they may be the same. I have worked with people who require millions of dollars in the bank to feel secure and satisfied in life; I have also coached people who live paycheck to paycheck and feel quite blessed.

Remember, wealth is more than just the sum of your dollars and cents. It is about living comfortably in your skin, experiencing happiness in your relationships, and feeling satisfied with the direction of your life. Wealth is personal and something that you alone must define for yourself.

Coaching Exercise #1:   A Wealthy You

Purpose:

This exercise helps you develop a personalized definition of what it means to be wealthy. When you truly understand and clarify your end goal, you are better equipped to take small steps toward achieving your vision.

Getting Started:

You will need 15-30 minutes to complete this exercise. You will also need a quiet comfortable place, a blank piece of paper or notebook if you don't want to write in this workbook, a pen or pencil, and your imagination.

Activity:

Imagine a day in your life as a wealthy person. Start the exercise with your alarm clock going off in the morning and then imagine your day as it unfolds, hour by hour.

What would your life look like, smell like, and taste like if you were truly wealthy? What activities would you be engaged in? Where would you be doing these activities? Who would you be spending time with? Who would not be in your wealthy life? How would you know you are wealthy?

Now take five to ten minutes to write about your experience. You may want to answers the above questions to help you get started. Include any information that you think is important from your visualization. Some people will write down the entire experience, others will jot down only a few words, and others will use pictures and images to tell their story. Do what makes sense to you. If you need more room, use the blank space at the end of this activity.

_____

_____

_____

_____

_____

_____

_____

_____

_____

_____

Now take a moment to reflect on your answers and this experience. When you are ready, write your two to three sentence definition of wealth below:

My Definition of Wealth is_____

_____

_____

_____

_____

_____

_____

_____

_____

Action & Accountability:

What action will you take based on this coaching activity?

Some examples include living by my wealth definition for a day or noticing when my financial habits are not helping me work toward my definition of a wealthy life.

_____

_____

_____

_____

_____

_____

_____

When will you take this action? In:

☐ 1 Day ☐ 1 Week ☐ 30 Days ☐ 60 Days ☐ Not Taking Action Now

Who will be your accountability partner?

_____

Now that you have a working definition of wealth, you are ready to explore your Money History. Remember to work at your own pace. If you need more time to contemplate this first coaching exercise, give yourself the time to do this work before moving on to the next chapter.

Chapter 2:   Accept Your Money History

Now that you have a personalized definition of wealth, it is time to start looking at how you can create more wealth in your life.

The first step in the **ABCs** of *Creating Wealth from the Inside Out* is called **Accept.** In order to move on to the healthy and wealthy future that awaits you, you'll need to come to terms with the past by accepting your money history, identifying your money scripts, and learning from your past financial experiences. While this may sound overwhelming at first, you will discover that tapping into your unconscious money beliefs is easier, and sometimes more fun, than you think.

Money Scripts

A money script is a thought or belief about money. Like a movie script tells an actor what to say and how to behave in each scene, a money script dictates what you say and how you behave around money in a particular situation. Your money scripts were developed during your childhood as you observed your parents, caregivers, and loved ones handle financial matters. Because these scripts were formed in your mind as a child when you could not fully appreciate the complexities of life, they are often oversimplified generalizations that are not true in all situations.

The tricky part about discovering your money scripts is that while some reside in your conscious mind, many exist just below the surface in your subconscious. Both types of money scripts impact your financial decision making on a daily basis. It is imperative to bring your money scripts to your conscious awareness so that you can make better financial decisions. If the particular script imparts a money rule or belief that makes good financial sense in a current circumstance, then abide by it. But if it is leading you to be overly emotional or to think in all or nothing terms, it may be a rule to consider modifying or disregarding all together.

The Classic Under Earner: Chad

Here is an example of how a money script can negatively impact your financial life.

> Chad is a hard-working, engineer who is good at his job. For years he has worked for a small company where he is underpaid. He believes that he deserves more money, but fears asking for a raise as he does not want to work longer hours. Chad wants to spend more time with his family, not less, so he does not talk to his boss about his salary. Instead he continues to under earn.

> Chad's money script, "Getting more money means working more hours," is causing Chad to avoid requesting adequate compensation for his experience level and his work performance. This script is based on watching his dad work long hours to make more money for the family. The difference is Chad's father was a laborer paid by the hour. The only way for his father to make more money was to work more hours. The same facts are simply not true in Chad's case and in his career. However, until Chad identifies and alters this money script, he will find it difficult to

find a job that pays him market rate or to ask his current employer for more money.

To successfully change your relationship with money, you need to discover your money scripts and how each one impacts your financial behaviors and well-being. Once these money messages are in your conscious awareness you can then decide whether to listen to them or not. Until you identify these beliefs, you will find making lasting change in your financial habits challenging.

How can you tune into your money scripts and bring them to your conscious awareness? The following coaching exercises will help you get started.

Coaching Exercise #2:   Your Money Scripts

Purpose:

The goal of this coaching exercise is to uncover more of your thoughts and beliefs about money. By bringing new money scripts to the surface, you can then decide which money messages you want to keep and which ones you want to let go of going forward.

Getting Started:

You will need 10 minutes to complete this exercise.

Activity:

Complete the following sentences with the first thought that comes into your mind. Do not censor your responses or worry whether or not your answers are politically correct. Go with your initial reaction and do not judge your answers. Just notice what thoughts and beliefs surface as you complete this exercise.

1. Wealthy people are_____

2. Poor people are _____

3. What my mother taught me about money was_____

4. What my father taught me about money was_____

5. The reason I do not have more money is_____

6. Asking people for money is_____

7. Talking about money is_____

8. The relationship between love and money is_____

_____

9. The relationship between spirituality/religion and money is _____

_____

10. People who pay retail prices are _____

11. People who will only buy items on sale are _____

12. Financial freedom means_____

13. Retirement means_____

14. The biggest financial lesson I want to teach my children or young people in my life is_____

15. My current relationship with money can be described as _____

_____

16. My partner's current relationship with money can be described as_____

_____

17. When I pay bills, I _____

18. When I save money, I _____

19. People who ask what things costs and other people's salaries are_____

_____

20. The biggest lie I tell myself about money is_____

_____

Take a moment to read your answers. How does each money script influence your current spending, saving, investing, and charitable giving habits? Write down your insights below:

_____
_____
_____
_____
_____
_____
_____
_____
_____
_____
_____
_____
_____

Action & Accountability:

What action are you willing to take as a result of this coaching activity?

Examples include giving this questionnaire to my romantic or business partner as a way of finding out his or her money scripts or noticing each time one of these beliefs comes up in my daily life.

_____

_____

_____

_____

When will you take this action? In:

☐ 1 Day   ☐ 1 Week   ☐ 30 Days   ☐ 60 Days   ☐ Not Taking Action Now

Who will be your accountability partner?

_____

If you want to delve deeper into your money scripts, continue on to the next coaching exercise. Otherwise, take time to let what you discovered about your thoughts and beliefs about money settle. When you feel ready, complete the next coaching activity.

Coaching Exercise #3:   Turn Up the Volume

Purpose:

The human brain has a wonderful ability to focus on a particular item once you tell it to do so.   This brain function is called the Reticular Activating System and it can be used to help you turn up the volume on your money scripts. By noticing your money messages daily, you can collect useful data to help you shift your money mindset to support more wealth.

Getting Started:

This coaching exercise will take one week to complete. While this may seem like a long time, it is important to invest this time and attention to discovering your money scripts if you are truly going to change your relationship with money.   You will need a pencil or pen to jot down your observations and a small notebook.

Activity:

For one week carry your money log or small notebook with you in your purse or briefcase. Jot down your thoughts and feelings any time you engage in any money-related activity.   At the end of the week, review your notes. Notice any trends in your thought patterns and highlight your most prominent money scripts. Also note any common themes you noticed during the exercise.

Here is an example of a partially completed money log:

MONDAY:
Bought new outfit for work; felt guilty and anxious as I paid for it.
"It was not on sale therefore, I paid too much."

Deposited money into my Roth IRA; felt great and proud.
"Wise people save money for retirement."

Paid monthly bills while watching TV; anxious and distracted.
"I hate paying bills"

TUESDAY:
New catalog came in the mail. Wish I could buy more clothes for work. Fear and sadness.
"Can't spend any more money on myself."

Boss wants to do my annual review. FEAR.
"I am so underpaid, but I can't ask for more money. He may fire me."

WEDNESDAY:
Car making a noise on the way to work. Dread. Fear. Anger.
"I can't afford a new car."

THURSDAY:
Husband and I discussed idea of getting a new car. Fought.
"Couples always fight about big purchases."

Review with boss. Got cost of living raise. Sadness and Relief.
"Can't ask for more. I am lucky to have a job."

FRIDAY:
Deposited paycheck in the bank. Felt great to have more money in my account.
"A penny earned is a penny saved."

Went out to dinner with my husband. Enjoyed it, but felt guilt and shame when the bill came.
"We spent too much and did not deserve to treat ourselves so well."

Money Scripts: "You need to deserve to spend money."
                "A penny earned is a penny saved."
                "Couples fight about major purchases."
                "Asking for money is not possible."
                "Wise people save for retirement."
                "Saving money is good."

Themes: Fear, guilt, and conflict over spending money. Saving money is a noble thing to do.

This journaling exercise helps you turn up the volume on your money scripts by bringing money beliefs into your conscious thought. The more you tap into your money scripts, the more opportunities you have to change or to let go of beliefs that do not serve you.

Action & Accountability:

What action are you willing to take as a result of this coaching activity?

Examples include continuing to note money scripts when I am shopping, identifying and sitting with the feelings related to a money habit, or picking one theme and journaling more in-depth about it.

_____

_____

_____

_____

_____

_____

_____

_____

_____

_____

When will you take this action? In:

☐ 1 Day   ☐ 1 Week   ☐ 30 Days ☐ 60 Days   ☐ Not Taking Action Now

Who will be your accountability partner?

_____

You have done some great work identifying and labeling your money scripts in this chapter. Take time to congratulate yourself on a job well done! Now that you have developed an ability to notice your thoughts about spending, saving, investing, and giving, noticing money scripts will be much easier.

Are you ready to learn about the various factors that influenced your money personality? If so, it is time to read the next chapter, Your Money Mindset.

Chapter 3:   Your Money Mindset

The sum of all your money scripts equals your money mindset. Your money mindset is influenced by a variety of factors including your family, your culture, your age, your gender, your economic social class, and your personal financial experiences. Below is a brief description of each one:

Family History: How your parents and caregivers handled financial matters during your childhood greatly affects your financial decision-making as an adult. Research shows that your money personality is primarily formed by 14 years of age. This highlights how influential your formative years are on your money mindset.

Culture: Your culture impacts your beliefs about money and its purpose in the world. If you were raised in the consumer driven economy of the United States, you grew up bombarded with media images and advertisements promoting the idea that the man (or woman) with the most toys wins. If you were raised in Europe, The Middle East, or China, your cultural money messages are very different.

Gender: Traditionally boys are raised to be competitive, to make money, and to be good providers in adulthood. Women are reared first to be good caregivers, to support the family, and to help others while putting their needs, monetary and otherwise, second. While these traditional roles are changing in the modern family, the money messages associated with gender run deep making your gender an important factor in your money mindset.

Age: The generation you belong to colors your perspective about money and wealth. If you were born during the Great Depression, your view of banks and saving money are very dissimilar than if you were born during the Baby Boom generation. A common money script of the baby boomer generation is "Rich people can't be trusted." Conversely, later generations such as those reared in the 1980's, heard the money message, "Greed is good."

Economic Social Class: The economic social class you were born into also influences your money mindset. If you were born into an affluent family, chances are you view money and its purpose in life dramatically different than if you were raised in poverty in the inner city.

Religion: Religion and money have an interesting, sometimes strained relationship. No matter what your religious upbringing or current affiliation, religion has a bearing on your money scripts. For example, the Biblical scripture that states, "The love of money is the root of all evil," has had a powerful effect on Christians and how they view wealth versus poverty. In Christianity, it is noble to be poor. Conversely, in Judaism the accumulation of wealth is not evil so long as wealth is used wisely.

Personal Financial Experiences: Personal money experiences, whether viewed as positive or negative, impact your money mindset. Significant events such as winning the lottery, receiving a sizable inheritance, filing for bankruptcy, going through an expensive divorce, or being laid off leave a lasting mark on your money psyche and ultimately alter your money scripts. Each of these events comes with a variety of mixed emotions that need to be understood and eventually integrated into your mindset.

Coaching Exercise #4:   Your Family Money Messages

Purpose:

The goal of this exercise is to help you look at your family's history around money through visual means and to examine how your unique heritage shaped your relationship with money and wealth. The information discovered should not be used to place blame on family members for your money mindset, but as a tool for gaining additional insights into your financial thoughts, feelings, and behaviors.

Getting Started:

This coaching exercise will take approximately 30 minutes to complete. You will need a large sheet of blank paper, a pencil, an eraser, and a ruler.

Activity:

A money tree is essentially a diagram that is focused on how each person in a family thinks, feels, and acts around money and how those financial mindsets and patterns are passed down generation to generation. It is a great tool to use to identify and display family patterns related to work, money, and wealth relatively quickly. It's like a family tree except instead of tracing bloodlines, you're diagramming the transmission of money messages.

Below is an example of a completed money tree:

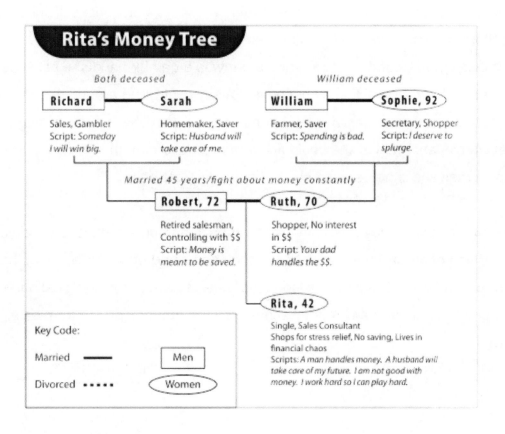

Rita's Money Tree

Both deceased

William deceased

Richard ——— Sarah

William ——— **Sophie, 92**

Sales, Gambler
Script: *Someday I will win big.*

Homemaker, Saver
Script: *Husband will take care of me.*

Farmer, Saver
Script: *Spending is bad.*

Secretary, Shopper
Script: *I deserve to splurge.*

Married 45 years/fight about money constantly

Robert, 72 ——— Ruth, 70

Retired salesman,
Controlling with $$
Script: *Money is meant to be saved.*

Shopper, No interest in $$
Script: *Your dad handles the $$.*

Rita, 42

Single, Sales Consultant
Shops for stress relief, No saving, Lives in financial chaos
Scripts: *A man handles money. A husband will take care of my future. I am not good with money. I work hard so I can play hard.*

Key Code:

Married ———

Divorced •••••

Men

Women

Summary: Rita has a conflicted relationship with dad and has been shopping with mom since she was very young. Shopping is Ruth's, Rita's mom, only coping strategy and way of expressing independence from Robert. Rita still shops with her mom Ruth on a weekly basis for "fun" and watches her mom hide her purchases from Robert.   Rita's grandfather was a gambler and she believes her dad reacted to his gambling by becoming overly controlling around money.   Rita wants to be more responsible with her money, is upset she is not in a long-term relationship, and wishes she could find a man to take over the finances. She also worries she is not "a good catch" because of her debt.

Now fill out your money tree. Make note of each person's occupation and your impression of his or her viewpoint on money and its purpose in life. If you have a blended family, make sure to include step-parents as well as biological parents in your chart. Next, note any money scripts you remember learning from each individual.

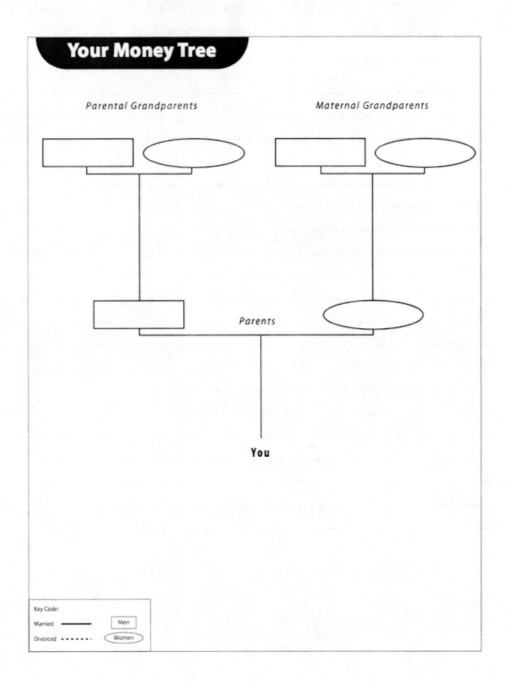

Take five minutes to journal write about your experience in the space provided below. What did you discover in completing your money tree? What did you learn about your history that was a surprise? What did you notice that helped make sense of how you are with money today?

_____

_____

_____

_____

_____

_____

_____

_____

_____

_____

_____

_____

_____

_____

_____

_____

_____

_____

_____

Once you complete the initial money tree, you may want to return and update the information as you learn more about your family's money history and messages. You may want to go back another generation by adding your maternal and paternal great grandparents. You many want to extend your chart by adding siblings, significant others, and children. By adding these members to your family tree, you can gain even more insight into your relationship with money and how it was shaped by the generations before you.

Action & Accountability:
What action are you willing to take as a result of this coaching activity?

Examples include sharing your money tree with your spouse, partner, or wealth coach or adding another generation to your chart.

_____
_____
_____
_____
_____

When will you take this action? In:
☐ 1 Day   ☐ 1 Week   ☐ 30 Days   ☐ 60 Days   ☐ Not Taking Action Now

Who will be your accountability partner for this action step?
_____

Looking at your family and its money history takes time. You may need a break after completing your money tree. If so, reward yourself with a well-deserved time out. When you are ready to dig a little deeper into your money mindset, move onto and complete the next coaching exercise.

Coaching Exercise #5:   Your Money Personality

Purpose:

This coaching activity helps you gain additional insight into the many factors that shape your money mindset.

Getting Started:

Set aside 30 to 45 minutes to do this entire coaching activity or if you prefer, set aside 5 to 10 minutes a day for the next six days.

Activity:

Answer the following questions as honestly and openly as possible. Your answers will give you more awareness of the many influences contributing to your money mindset. Feel free to skip a question if it does not apply to you.

How did the culture you were born into shape your thoughts and beliefs about money? What cultural traditions and beliefs do you want to keep and why? Which ones do you want to let go of?

_____
_____
_____
_____
_____
_____
_____
_____
_____
_____
_____
_____
_____

What ideas about work, money, and wealth were encouraged in your generation? How does this generational money philosophy help you maintain a healthy, wealthy lifestyle? How does it get in the way?

_____
_____
_____
_____
_____
_____
_____
_____
_____
_____
_____
_____
_____
_____

What gender stereotypes were you taught, either verbally or by observation, and how have these lessons impacted your money mindset?

_____
_____
_____
_____
_____
_____
_____
_____
_____

_____

_____

_____

_____

_____

_____

How does your social class (working class, middle class, middle upper class, or affluent) impact your money thoughts, beliefs, and habits? What money scripts and money habits from this social class work for you? What thoughts and behaviors do not?

_____

_____

_____

_____

_____

_____

_____

_____

_____

_____

_____

What religious and spiritual beliefs were you raised with and how do these teachings impact your relationship with money?

_____

_____

_____

_____

_____

_____

_____

_____

_____

_____

_____

_____

_____

_____

_____

What significant personal money events (losing a job, winning the lottery, inheriting money, declaring bankruptcy, going into foreclosure, etc.) have you experienced in your lifetime? How have these experiences shaped your relationship with money and wealth?

_____

_____

_____

_____

_____

_____

_____

_____

_____

_____

_____

_____

_____

_____

_____

_____

_____

Action & Accountability:

What action are you willing to take as a result of this coaching activity?

Examples include continuing to journal on a particular question, talking to my partner or money coach about my answers, or actively working to replace an unhealthy money script with a new one.

_____

_____

_____

_____

_____

When will you take this action? In:

☐ 1 Day ☐ 1 Week ☐ 30 Days ☐ 60 Days ☐ Not Taking Action Now

Who will be your accountability partner for this action step?

_____

Congratulations! You have completed a large piece of money coaching work. You have identified your money scripts, examined your family's money messages, and looked at how all your unique life experiences with money have shaped your money mindset.   Celebrate and reward yourself for all your hard work. You deserve it.

Now that you have identified and worked on accepting your money history, it is time to move on to the next step in the **ABCs** of _Creating Wealth from the Inside Out_ process. It is time to **Believe.**

Chapter 4:   Believe in Your Worth

The second step in the **ABC's** of *Creating Wealth from the Inside Out* is **Believe**. To create a wealthy life you need to believe in yourself and feel deep down inside that you are worth taking care of financially. While this sounds simple, it is often the most complicated part of wealth coaching process.

Believing in oneself is also known as self-esteem. It is defined as having confidence in your abilities and pride. It is not static, but an ever-changing state. Someone with a healthy self-esteem feels good and satisfied with himself or herself most of the time.   A person who struggles with low self-esteem is more reactive to the environment, finds it hard to practice self-care, and is often unsatisfied in life.

What does self-esteem have to do with creating wealth in your life? Everything! People who mismanage money, ignore finances, under earn, over spend or don't save, or who otherwise don't take adult responsibility around money in their life have one thing in common: Low self-esteem. Some feel unworthy of receiving wealth, while others feel that financial security is not possible. If you fall into one of these categories, it is okay. Just like you can alter your relationship with money, you can change and increase your self-esteem.

The Poor Rich Boy: Jon

The following case study illustrates how low self-worth can limit your ability to make and manage money responsibly.

Jon, a 28-year old young man from an affluent family, started coaching with me at the recommendation of his financial advisor. The advisor's referral was born out of his frustration with his client as he viewed Jon as highly intelligent, but unmotivated. The advisor stated that "He refuses to change his spending habits and I can't help him until he does."

Jon came to the initial session uncertain about wealth coaching. He shared that he wanted to figure out why he threw money away, but felt like he was a hopeless case. "My mom and dad are frustrated with my mismanagement of money as well. No matter what I do people seem to be disappointed in me."

I assured Jon that our work would be to uncover the reasons for his fiscal problems and that no matter what the outcome, I would not be disappointed. My only expectation was for him to show up and participate in our sessions. He seemed relieved knowing that I was not going to judge him based on his progress in this area.

Over the course of the first several appointments, Jon and I explored his relationship to money, his experience growing up in a wealthy family, and his apparent struggle to follow a reasonable financial plan. His father was a very successful, high-powered business executive who sold his company for a very large sum a few years after Jon was born. From a very early age, Jon knew that he would inherit a great deal of wealth. On the surface he talked about this being a great thing – not having to work, not having to worry about his future, and not having to think about what he would like to do after graduate school. However, in our time together it became clear to me that Jon's inherited wealth was a burden.

When we looked at the idea that being a wealthy heir was not all it was cracked up to be, Jon realized that he did not feel he deserved the wealth and he did not feel very good about himself as a person. "What have I done other than be born to have this money?" For the first time, Jon openly expressed his mixed feelings regarding his family's affluence. He felt guilty hanging out all day while his friends were at work. Often, he would spend money on his friends to gain their approval as he feared if he did not pick up the bill or buy his friends lavish gifts they would leave him. Jon had confused his self-worth with his net-worth.

Jon's feelings of unworthiness resulted in him haphazardly spending money. He realized through coaching that giving money away was an attempt to feel better about himself and in his mind, "to make up for being a trust fund baby." While it was an unconscious attempt to feel better, living in financial chaos, and disappointing his parents only made him feel worse.

Once he labeled his money scripts and his feelings, Jon started to reframe his thoughts about himself and his worth in the world. He discovered that although he did not need to work, he wanted to. With time and support, he found a job he loved at a technology company. Working as a productive member of society resulted in him feeling better about his purpose in life and enabled him to build an identity separate from his family's legacy. In time, he slowed down his excess spending and made real progress in learning how to manage his money in a more responsible, mature way.

Jon is a great example of how money scripts about self-worth can block you from accumulating or managing money on a day-to-day basis. His low self-esteem, conflicted feelings about his inheritance, and his failure to consciously connect his thoughts about money to his unhealthy financial habits all contributed to his constant state of financial upheaval. It was not until he truly believed in his worth as a person that he could make lasting behavioral change in his relationship with money.

A Word of Caution

Sometimes low self-esteem results in other destructive behaviors such as addictions, eating disorders, depression, and abusive relationships. These psychiatric problems can occur separately from or as part of a money disorder. If you struggle with one of these serious emotional issues, I strongly encourage you to consider psychotherapy as coaching alone is not an adequate tool to address these types of personal issues.

Now that you understand how self-esteem, believing in your worth, and financial habits are related, let's take a moment to rate your self-esteem.

Coaching Exercise #6:   Your Self-Esteem

Purpose:

This coaching activity is designed to determine areas where your self-esteem is strong and places where it may need some boosting.

Getting Started:

This coaching exercise will take about 10 minutes to complete.

Activity:

Take a moment to read and answer the following true or false statements. Write a "T" if the statement is true and an "F" if the statement is false.

_____ 1. I am willing to take risks.

_____ 2. My income is tied to my self-confidence.

_____ 3. I like myself most of the time.

_____ 4. I get angry that I'm not thinner, smarter, or more financially successful.

_____ 5. Growing up, I knew I was a good person.

_____ 6. I do not bounce back easily after failure.

_____ 7. I am likely to ask for support from others.

_____ 8. I would be happier if I made over $100,000.

_____ 9. I look people in the eye when I am talking to them.

_____ 10. I am confident I can improve my relationship with money.

Now review your answers. A true response on the odd numbered questions indicates good self-esteem. A true response on the even numbered questions is indicative of someone who needs to improve his or her self-esteem. A person with high self-worth will have mostly true responses on the odd numbered statements and very few true responses on the even ones.

Use your answers as a guide to examine your current self-esteem. Take a moment to identify the areas you need to work on to feel more confident and to validate the areas where your self-esteem is strong.

Action & Accountability:
What action are you willing to take as a result of this coaching activity?

Examples include attending a self-esteem workshop, repeating daily affirmations about your worth as a person, or seeing a coach or therapist to find strategies to improve your self-concept.

_____

_____

_____

_____

_____

When will you take this action? In:

☐ 1 Day   ☐ 1 Week   ☐ 30 Days   ☐ 60 Days   ☐ Not Taking Action Now

Who will be your accountability partner for this action step?

_____

Building and maintaining high self-esteem is an on-going process. You can exercise and strengthen your self-worth muscle while continuing your money coaching journey or you can take a detour and then come back to the work. Check in and see what feels right for you. When it makes sense, move on to the next chapter, Shift Your Money Mindset, and learn a simple and effective technique for changing unhealthy money scripts.

Chapter 5:   Shift Your Money Mindset

Changing your money habits starts with shifting your money mindset to include thoughts and beliefs that support healthy financial behaviors. The best method for doing this cognitive work is The Mind Over Money Method (MOMM). This technique is based on the theory that in any given situation you have automatic thoughts (AT), automatic feelings (AF), and automatic behaviors (AB) that dictate how you act. Each time you face the same situation, these thoughts, feelings, and behaviors are experienced again and reinforced.

With enough repetition, you develop a belief about the situation and start to predict outcomes based on past experience. Often this entire sequence happens quickly and unconsciously, making the outcome appear to be something that you cannot control. However, if we identify our automatic thoughts, we can change our feelings, our behaviors, and the outcome. If you use The Mind Over Money Method, you can shift your money mindset!

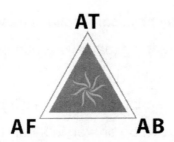

Diagram of Automatic Thoughts (AT), Automatic Feelings (AF), and Automatic Behaviors (AB)

The Mind Over Money Method (MOMM)

MOMM involves 6 steps; each one is detailed below. Using this technique helps you alter money scripts that contribute to harmful and damaging money habits.

Step 1:   Identify the situation or event that results in an unwanted financial outcome.

Step 2:   Identify your automatic thoughts (AT) about the situation.

Step 3:   Identify the automatic feelings (AF) you experience related to each of the automatic thoughts.

Step 4:   Identify the automatic behaviors (AB) you experience during this event. Include any physical reactions or sensations like your heart racing, pulse increasing, palms sweating, etc . . .

Step 5:   Test each money script to determine if it is a fact or a belief. A fact is statement that can be proven in a court of law to be true. Facts are supported by hard evidence that proves it's universally true. Be careful as money beliefs run deep and sometimes feel like facts even when they are really just beliefs.

Step 6:   Take each belief and challenge it by asking the following questions:
1. What makes this belief true?
2. What makes this belief false?
3. How does this money script support my financial health?
4. How does this money script get in the way of my financial health?
5. What is a different way of looking at the situation?
6. How does this new perspective change your feelings, reactions, and ultimate financial decisions and habits?

Now come up with a new, more balanced view of the situation that ultimately will support a more financially healthy mindset or habit. This last step is the most challenging and working with an experienced wealth coach can be very helpful.

The Ultimate Saver: Jennifer

Here is a case illustration of MOMM in action.

As a child, Jennifer received a weekly allowance from her parents. Every week she took great pride in filling out her deposit slip and putting the money in her passport savings account. Jennifer loved the bank and the way the tellers would treat her as an adult during each transaction. On the way home, her dad would always ask if she wanted to buy anything with her allowance like a toy or some penny candy. Jennifer would shake her head "no" and her dad would exclaim, "What a good little saver you are! " This series of events was played out over and over again and her thoughts, feelings, and behaviors were always the same. Eventually, Jennifer developed the money scripts, "It feels good to save," and "People like me when I save money."

While saving is a healthy financial practice, being able to spend money is also part of a well-balanced financial life. By the time I met Jennifer she was 32 and had a great deal of trouble buying anything she viewed as not necessary. She was so restrictive in her spending that she did not own a box spring or headboard for her bed because in her mind, she could simply sleep on the mattress on the floor. She made a large salary as a physician's assistant, but did not allow herself any monetary joy. In fact, she denied herself all the pleasures that come with being single, in a city, and working in a large hospital. She declined social invitations as going out to eat was costly and missed out on many other opportunities for the same reason.

Jennifer knew something was wrong with her relationship with money but was very confused because her excessive saving was always viewed by others so favorably. When she became depressed and more isolated she decided to reach out for help. Her financial advisor referred her to KBK Wealth Connection for coaching. The first week she came into my office I taught her the MOMM method. Here is what her worksheet looked like:

Step 1: Identify the Situation: Inability to spending money on myself leading to unhappiness and isolation.

Step 2: Automatic Thoughts: Money should be saved. It is bad to spend. I will get out of control. Savings is a good practice.

Step 3: Automatic Feelings: Fear, anxiety, and shame

Step4: Automatic Behaviors: Heart races, sweaty palms

Step 5: Test AT/Money Scripts   Money should be saved. – Belief
It is bad to spend. – Belief
I will get out of control. – Belief
Saving is a good practice. - Fact

Step 6: Challenge Beliefs   Money should be saved is all-or-nothing thinking. Sometime you need to spend money. It is not necessarily bad to spend money, sometimes is a wise financial action. I have never gotten out of control with money. I may feel out of control but that does not mean I will definitely get out of control.

More balanced money script: Saving and spending money is part of the ebb and flow of life and I deserve to take care of myself by both having a savings account for the future and having a spending allowance for buying non-essential items and having fun in the here and now.

Notice how Jennifer's new money script is less childlike, less all-or-nothing, and more in line with a balanced healthy adult life. While Jennifer's money scripts and habits were firmly entrenched and required longer term coaching, she eventually mastered the Mind Over Money Method and could quickly adjust her perspective outside our sessions. She eventually bought herself a bedroom set and worked with a financial planner to determine how much disposable income she had to work with each month. She became less isolated, started going out more with friends, and found that embracing money as something that ebbs and flows allowed her to be more flexible in other areas of her life as well.

If you are ready to put what you just learned into practice, move on to the next coaching exercise, Your Mind Over Money.

Coaching Exercise #7:   Your Mind Over Money

Purpose:

This coaching exercise is designed to teach you the Mind Over Money Method (MOMM). You may want to complete this activity a few times as it takes repetition to learn and integrate this technique into your thought process.

Getting Started:

This coaching exercise will take 30 minutes to complete.

The first time you use MOMM, it may be a bit overwhelming, so you may want to enlist some help from a trained professional wealth coach or cognitive behavioral therapist. Know that with practice and support, this technique will free you from unhealthy financial attitudes and habits.

Activity:

Take a moment and think of the last time you engaged in a financial situation that left you feeling unhappy or resulted in a negative consequence. When you have a scenario in mind, complete the following exercise based on the MOMM method.   If you get stuck at any point, ask a trusted friend, a wealth coach, or a financial therapist to help you.

Step 1: Situation: _____

Step 2: Identify your automatic thoughts (AT):

_____

_____

_____

_____

_____

Step 3: Identify your automatic feelings (AF):

_____

_____

_____

_____

_____

Step 4: Identify your automatic behaviors (AB):

_____

_____

_____

_____

_____

Step 5: Test your automatic thoughts and put each one in the appropriate column under "Facts" or "Beliefs" below. If you are uncertain, put the thought in the belief column for now as further questions in Step 6 will clarify it for you.

BELIEFS:	FACTS:
Ex. I should save money.	Saving money is a sound financial habit.

Step 6: Challenge each belief. How else could you view the situation?

BELIEF:	NEW PERSPECTIVE:
Ex. I should save money.	I like to save money, but it's not a "should," it's a "want."

When you have completed Steps 1 through 6, review the entire exercise again. Now write a more balanced way of viewing the situation that will support a positive financial and/or emotional impact.

My new, more balanced money script:

_____

_____

_____

_____

_____

_____

_____

_____

_____

_____

Action & Accountability:

What action will you take as a result of this coaching activity?

Examples include doing a MOMM exercise each day or repeating my new healthy money script each morning.

_____

_____

_____

_____

When will you take this action? In:

☐ 1 Day   ☐ 1 Week   ☐ 30 Days   ☐ 60 Days   ☐ Not Taking Action Now

Who will be your accountability partner for this action step?

_____

Now that you have a tool for shifting your money mindset, let's look at how individuals change habits.

Chapter 6:   Are You Ready to Change?

Financial change happens in the same way as any other behavioral change – one step at a time. Knowing how people typically change habits will help you determine if you are truly ready for the challenge of shifting your money mindset.

The Stages of Financial Change

The following outlines the five stages of change individuals typically pass through when altering a financial habit. These stages are based on the research conducted by Prohaska and DiClemente at the University of Rhode Island.

The Five Stages of Change

1. Pre-contemplation
2. Contemplation
3. Preparation
4. Action
5. Maintenance

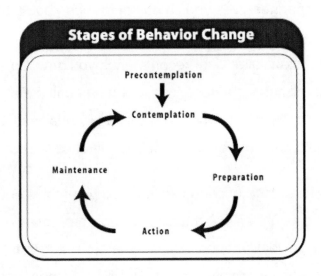

Pre-contemplation: You are in the pre-contemplation stage when you are aware of the need to change, but are not motivated to do so. You may be pressured by significant others to change your financial behaviors or you may be forced to examine your financial situation as a result of an event, such as a death in the family, the birth of a child, or the sale of a business. You may say to yourself, "I should settle my dad's estate," or "My wife and I should have a retirement plan," but you believe that settling the estate will be complicated and depressing or that you are too young to worry about retirement. If you are in the pre-contemplation phase, you defend the status quo and are not ready to make any substantial and lasting changes.

Examples of this stage include:

- Your partner gives you a copy of this workbook, but you have no desire to read it.
- Your financial advisor recommends you draw up an estate plan. You tell her it is a good idea, but never call the attorney.
- Your father dies, leaves you the family business, and you think, "I should learn more about business finance." You fail to follow-up.

Contemplation: This stage of change is marked by ambivalent feelings. You see your financial ways as unhealthy, realize you have a problem, and may even hire a financial advisor or wealth coach thinking you are ready to take action. What you do not realize—and therefore cannot tell others—is that you have strong feelings about altering your spending, saving, giving, and investing habits, and equally strong feelings about not altering them. For example, you may say that you want to save more money, but your spending habits, and therefore your savings account balance, remain unchanged. Intellectually you want to increase your savings, but emotionally you continue to spend since that is familiar and comfortable. Because taking action is uncomfortable in the short run, you continue to think about making change in the long run, but do not make any concrete shifts in your day-to-day financial behavior to achieve your goal.

Examples of this stage include:

- You visit your local bank and find out how to set up a savings account. You say you want to save more money, but decide not to set up the account.
- You think retirement planning is a good idea, but you miss the open enrollment period stating, "I just don't have enough to save right now."

- You hire a financial therapist to help you stop overspending. After three sessions you drop out because you find monitoring your spending in the short run annoying.

Preparation: Preparation is marked by a clear commitment to change. You may be working with a financial advisor or a wealth coach on changing your relationship to money. In addition to the coaching, you may be reading financial books, magazines or blogs, talking to friends about investing, taking financial literacy workshops, or actively engaged in planning discussions. Also known as the determination stage, this phase is marked by statements such as, "I will do better managing my money;" "I will listen to the professionals and follow their recommendations;" and "Tell me what to do and I will do it."

Examples of this stage include:

- You make an appointment with your human resource person to discuss retirement plans available at your company.
- You listen to the *Creating Wealth From The Inside Out Audio* and take notes on what you learn.
- You have a financial meeting with your spouse to discuss how you can both collect financial information over the next month so you can put a household budget together.

Action: Most of us want to be in the action stage from the start as it involves taking steps such as debt reduction, budgeting, and conscious financial planning—steps that reinforce your belief in your ability to make positive shifts in your financial life. However, you usually need to work through the other stages of change in order to truly be ready for meaningful action. Research shows that you will spend less time in this phase than any other. You can expect to be here for as little as an hour or as long as six months.

Examples of this stage include:

- Filling out and submitting the paper work for an automatic savings withdrawal to be made to your checking account monthly.
- Hiring a financial advisor.
- Meeting with an estate attorney and writing up an estate plan.

Maintenance: After you have altered your money habits, integration of your new behaviors is the primary goal. It is important for you to avoid temptations and be aware of triggers that cause you to revert to your old behaviors. At this stage, you should anticipate problematic money situations and how to handle them differently than in the past. Old money messages may pop up again, but if you continue to receive support and make adjustments when old habits surface, you will achieve long lasting financial change.

Examples of this stage include:

- You overspend on the weekend and on Monday you look at what triggered you emotionally to ignore your budget.
- You continue to contribute to your Roth Individual Retirement Account on a monthly basis.
- You see a pair of red cowboy boots and think, "I have to have them!" You take a deep breathe, slow down, and evaluate why you want to buy the shoes. You decide not to buy the boots as one pair of red boots seems like enough in your closet.

The Slippery Slope of Change

It is part of the change process to occasionally fall back into old, unhealthy behaviors. When you slip, do not throw in the towel. Instead pick yourself up, dust yourself off, and get support as soon as possible. Treat each setback as an opportunity to learn and grow. Only through learning from your money mistakes will you handle money differently going forward.

The World's Best Shopper: Tina

Tina is a wonderful illustration of how people's thoughts and feelings about money shift gradually.

> When Tina started coaching, she was one of the world's best shoppers. Always impeccably dressed, she loved fashion and spending money on clothes, shoes, and accessories. Her husband gave her an ultimatum the night before she called to make an appointment. She did not think her shopping was a problem, but her husband did and threatened to stop paying her credit card bills. It was clear in our initial session that Tina was firmly planted in the pre-contemplation stage of change. The only reason she was sitting in my office talking about her financial habits was her husband's insistence that she get help.
>
> Tina and I discussed her shopping routine, her history of buying clothes to feel less lonely, and how she binged on clothes just like she binged on food. I educated her about what it would take to stop her unhealthy behaviors and how she would need to look at her feelings as well as her behaviors around money. At the end of our time together, Tina set up a follow-up coaching appointment, but a few days later cancelled it. She was just not ready to change.

Three months after our initial meeting, Tina called my office in tears. She said, "When I am sad, I shop. When I am angry, I shop. When I am bored, I shop. All I do in life is shop!" She agreed to come in again and revisit the idea of working together.

This time Tina was more engaged in the process. She shared with me how she was frightened to let go of her numerous weekly trips to the mall and was also afraid of what would happen to her marriage and her financial situation if she did not. Tina was clearly on the fence about changing her behaviors and had moved into the contemplation stage of change. Together, we discussed that it was okay to receive coaching even if she was not 100% ready to make a change in her spending. She seemed relieved to know that I would not be pressuring her to stop spending like so many people in her life.

Over the course of our work together, Tina examined her money scripts, her family money messages, and how she learned to use shopping to cope with life's ups and downs. She learned how to slow down her knee jerk reaction to emotional events by heading to the mall and replacing it with deep breathing, journal writing, and positive self-talk. By discovering new coping skills, Tina had moved into the preparation stage of change. She was setting the stage for letting go of her destructive shopping behavior once and for all.

Shortly after, Tina moved into the action stage of change. She shopped less compulsively and eventually replaced this destructive habit with healthier ones. She identified the underlying psychological issues and entered marital therapy with her husband. When we last spoke, Tina was being more financially responsible. Also, she and her husband were saving for their first house.

We all change in stages. Identifying the stage of change you are in relative to a financial habit is empowering. This awareness leads you to take the necessary steps and get the support systems in place to ultimately take action on your financial goals.

To find out how you alter unwanted habits, continue on to the next coaching exercise.

Coaching Exercise #8: How You Change

Purpose:

In this coaching exercise, you discover data that will assist you in changing unwanted financial habits.

Getting Started:

This coaching exercise will take 10 to 15 minutes to complete.

Activity:

Ponder a time in your life when you have successfully changed an unwanted habit or behavior. Did you quit smoking, start exercising, stop swearing, or start a new meditation practice? Now that you have identified a situation, answer the following questions:

1. What was your habit like before you wanted to change?

   _____
   _____
   _____
   _____
   _____

2. What triggered a desire to change?

   _____
   _____
   _____
   _____
   _____

3. Was it a person, place, or thing that moved you to let go of this unhealthy behavior and/or start a new one?

_____
_____
_____
_____
_____

4. What was it like when you first started the process of change?

_____
_____
_____
_____
_____

5. What made changing the behavior difficult?

_____
_____
_____
_____
_____

6. What parts of engaging in a new behavior were easy or motivating?

_____
_____
_____
_____
_____

7. How did you integrate this new behavior into your life in a lasting way?

_____

_____

_____

_____

_____

Action & Accountability:

What action will you take as a result of this coaching activity?

Examples include looking at another example of how I changed a behavior to gather more insight or reading about the work of Prohaska and DiClemente, the pioneers of the stages of change model.

_____

_____

_____

_____

When will you take this action? In:

☐ 1 Day   ☐ 1 Week   ☐ 30 Days ☐ 60 Days   ☐ Not Taking Action Now

Who will be your accountability partner for this action step?

_____

Now let's find out what stage of change you are in relative to a particular financial situation or habit.

Coaching Exercise #9:   Your Stage of Change

Purpose:

To identify the stage of change you are currently in relative to a specific financial behavior.

Getting Started:

This coaching exercise will take 10 minutes to complete.

Activity:

Identify a financial behavior you would like to change in the next 60 days.

Targeted Financial Habit:

_____

Now take some time to think about what stage of change you are in relative to this habit? It may help to ask the following questions: Why do I want to change? Who wants me to change? How do I feel about this potential change?   What concrete steps have I taken to change?

Now check the appropriate box below.

___ Pre-contemplation (Ignorance is Bliss)

___ Contemplation (Sitting on the Fence)

___ Preparation (Testing the Waters)

___ Action (Actively changing a habit)

___ Maintenance (Integrated into your lifestyle)

What information can you use from Coaching Exercise #8, How You Change, to help you move forward on your goal to change this financial habit? Be specific.

_____

_____

_____

_____

_____

Action & Accountability:

What action are you going to take as a result of this coaching exercise?

Examples include writing a list of financial habits I would like to change and identifying the stage of change I am in relative to each one or communicating my desire to change this financial habit to a trusted friend, my partner, my financial advisor, and/or my wealth coach.

_____

_____

_____

_____

_____

_____

When will you take this action? In:

☐ 1 Day   ☐ 1 Week   ☐ 30 Days ☐ 60 Days   ☐ Not Taking Action Now

Who will be your accountability partner for this action step?

_____

Now that you identified your readiness to change your financial habits, it is time to move to the last step in the **ABCs** of *Creating Wealth from the Inside Out* process. It is time to **Create**.

Chapter 7:   Create Opportunities to Receive Wealth

Once you accept and learn from your money history, identify and shift your money mindset, and truly believe in your worth, you are ready for the last step in the **ABCs** of *Creating Wealth from the Inside Out* process. You are ready to **create** opportunities to receive wealth.

Creating opportunities to receive wealth means you have an abundant attitude toward your personal and professional life and you allow yourself to receive from others as freely as you allow yourself to give. Living from this positive perspective, the land of plenty, allows you to welcome additional emotional and financial resources into your daily experience. In the land of plenty, there is enough money to go around to meet everyone's needs.

If you just had a reaction while reading the last few paragraphs, you are not alone. Many of us were raised in the land of scarcity. The land of scarcity is defined as a place where you give more than you receive because your money scripts tell you there are not enough monetary and non-financial resources for everyone to prosper. This money mindset contributes to you earning less than you are worth and feeling noble as a result.   Unless you shift this scarcity mindset you will under earn, not actively seek out opportunities to receive wealth, and remain unhappy with your relationship with money.

The Classic Under Earner: Penny

Penny is a perfect example of someone who lives in the land of scarcity. She is a social worker from a working class family and grew up watching her parents really struggle financially. Her family money message was "Hard work and perseverance eventually pays off." Her father died before he reached his payoff and her mother is still working six days a week to make ends meet.

Penny went to college and received a graduate degree in social work. She got married in her thirties, had one child, and soon after, started her own private therapy practice. She loves helping people, but is frustrated with her lack of income and feels victimized by the healthcare system. At times, she secretly gets angry with her wealthier clients because she believes that people from affluent families are greedy and self-centered. Penny works hard in her practice and is angry about her financial situation, but takes no action to change her circumstances.

Like a lot of people in the helping professions, Penny is a classic example of an under earner living in the land of scarcity. Her attitude toward wealth results in her not charging more for her services, not being creative in how she runs her business, and feeling stuck and destined to work hard while hoping for a big payoff. A payoff that is highly unlikely to come to fruition with her current money mindset.

So how can you avoid Penny's fate? By cultivating an abundant money mindset.

Now let's talk about how you can put this theory into practice.

Practice Receiving

I call the act of welcoming wealth into your life, the art of practicing receiving. The term came from a friend of mine when she tried to treat me to lunch one day. She went to pick up the tab and I refused to let her pay. My money script, unconscious at the time, screamed, "I can't take money from friends." I could not tolerate what I felt emotionally when someone else paid for my lunch or anything for that matter. We fought over the bill for 5 minutes when finally my friend looked me in the eye and said, "Will you practice receiving?" We laughed out loud at how absurd the situation was and I let her pay.

I felt very uncomfortable when the waitress picked up the invoice and my friend used her money to pay for lunch. But I lived! From that day forward, "practice receiving" became a mantra of mine. I say it to myself when I need help tolerating the emotional discomfort I experience when someone pays my way. The good news is the more I practice receiving, the easier it becomes. And the same can be true for you!

Coaching Exercise #10:   Practice Receiving

Purpose:

Changing a behavior involves stepping outside your comfort zone and practicing a new strategy until you master it. This coaching exercise is designed to do just that when it comes to receiving wealth.

Getting Started:

Set aside 20 minutes to do this coaching exercise. You will need a pen or pencil, scissors, glue, a large white piece of paper, and some old magazines.

Activity:

Pick one of the following sentences to use in this coaching activity. Now set a timer and write for 5 minutes using the statement as a starting point. Do not edit yourself or try to come up with the "right" answer. Just let your mind wander.

- Receiving money is . . .
- Receiving help is . . .
- Receiving wealth is . . .

Now take the next 10 minutes and cut out pictures and words from old magazines that represent your thoughts and feelings about receiving money, help, or wealth. Notice any automatic thoughts, feelings, and attitudes toward receiving that surface during this coaching exercise. Use this written and visual information to identify and overcome any roadblocks to creating and receiving wealth.

Action & Accountability:

What action will you take as a result of this coaching exercise?

Examples include writing a list of 3 ways you can receive wealth next week and then practice receiving in these specific ways or repeating the mantra "I am practicing receiving" every time accepting wealth gets emotionally uncomfortable.

_____

_____

_____

_____

_____

When will you take this action? In:

☐ 1 Day ☐ 1 Week ☐ 30 Days ☐ 60 Days ☐ Not Taking Action Now

Who is my accountability partner for this action step?

_____

Now that you have completed the **ABC's** of _Creating Wealth from the Inside Out_, you are ready to start talking about money with others in your life. The next chapter teaches you the how, when, and where of financial conversations.

Chapter 8:   Financial Conversations

Few people find it easy to talk openly about money. Therefore, if you find financial conversations awkward and complicated, you are not alone. Money is still a taboo subject in our society with many of us from families who considered talking about money to be rude, inappropriate, and impolite.

Despite the pressure to remain silent about your finances, engaging in a money conversation is an important skill. You may prefer to skip this step, but the bottom line is with a little bit of insight and training you can master financial conversations. And when you discuss financial matters with ease and grace, you are in a better position to manage your finances, negotiate your salary, make wise investments decisions, and realize your definition of wealth.

The first step involves spending some time developing a relationship with your money. I know this sounds weird, but until you figure out how to talk to and listen to your money, you will have a hard time articulating your feelings, thoughts, and opinions to someone else. You will practice this skill in the next coaching exercise.

Once you have mastered talking to your own money, it will be time to engage in financial conversations with others. As with all types of communication, it is best to agree to some ground rules prior to the discussion. Here are a few that I recommend you consider:

Financial Conversation Guidelines

- <u>Be respectful:</u> It is always important to treat the other person in the conversation with respect. Listen actively (described below), do not interrupt, and refrain from using profanity or blaming language.

- <u>Use "I" statements:</u> Start the conversation with "I am concerned about X, Y, and Z," not "You did X, Y, and Z." It may feel like a subtle difference, but it will get both of you started off on the right foot.

- <u>Actively listen:</u> This type of listening involves paying attention to both verbal and non-verbal communication to find meaning in what your partner is saying. Learning this technique takes time; however, with a little practice it is a very effective way of engaging in a money conversation. The steps involved in active listening are:

    a. The speaker expresses an opinion.

    I think we should save more because we want to pay for the kids' college and I fear if we don't have an adequate savings fund that we will get into financial trouble.

    b. The listener then clarifies his or her perceptions of what is said.

    What I hear you saying is you want to save more to fund the kids' college education and to feel safer.

c. The speaker then restates essential points and ideas.

Yes and to also fund an emergency savings fund just in case. This would make me feel more secure about our financial future.

d. The listener then summarizes the content of the message to check validity and acknowledges the opinion and contribution of the speaker.

You want to save more money for the kids' college, to fund an emergency fund, and to feel more secure about our financial future. Thank you for sharing your thoughts with me.

- <u>Practice curiosity:</u> Go into the conversation with a healthy dose of curiosity. Pretend you are a scientist interviewing a subject for a research project. Ask thoughtful questions to learn more about your partner's viewpoint. When you are truly curious you learn more and you are too busy wondering to pick a fight!

- <u>Don't mind read:</u> It is important to ask your partner what his or her intentions are or were around spending, saving, gifting, or investing money. Do not assume you know. You may make an educated guess, but it will be based on your money scripts not your partners. Jumping to conclusions and reading the other person's mind can result in frustration and anger that is unproductive and often unfounded. Do yourself and your partner a favor and don't read minds.

Financial conversations can get emotional because money taps into our primitive sense of security in the world.   Tread lightly and agree to disagree before you engage in a money dialogue. The goal is to understand each other's viewpoint, to keep an open mind, and to lay the groundwork for more financial dialogues in the future.

At the end of every financial meeting, make sure you build in a reward for taking this pro-active step toward wealth and wellness. Coupling a positive experience with a money dialogue will reinforce that talking about money is an important and enjoyable experience.

Coaching Exercise #11:   Talk to Your Money

Purpose:

The goal of this coaching exercise is to develop a relationship with your money and continue to identify your thoughts, beliefs, and feelings about it.

Getting Started:

This coaching exercise will take approximately 30 minutes to complete. You will need a blank piece of notebook paper and a pen or a pencil.

Activity:

Start by taking your clean sheet of note paper and writing "Dear Money" at the top. For the next 10 minutes, I want you to write a letter to your money as if it were a person. It is important to just begin the letter with whatever comes to mind, even if it does not make sense. I am purposefully not going to ask you guided questions as I want this letter to evolve organically. Trust me the experience will be richer as a result.

As you work on your letter, remind yourself that there is no correct way to do this coaching activity. Do not judge what you are writing. Do not worry about grammar, spelling, or punctuation. Just write in free form and let your thoughts take you where they want to go.

When you are finished, write down two or three emotions you experienced while drafting the letter. It may help to re-read the letter and then check in with yourself to label what feelings are present for you.

When you are done with the first letter, turn your piece of paper over and write a response letter from money to you for the next 10 minutes. At the top, write "Dear (Your Name)." Once again, let you mind wander, do not judge, and take time at the end to check in and see what you are feeling about the experience. When you are done with this second letter, write down two to three emotions that you experienced during this part of the exercise.

Here is an example from one of my wealth coaching clients to help you understand how writing a letter to money works:

Dear Money,

When I was a young girl I loved you. I loved counting you, playing with my cash register, and handling you. When I grew up I learned that loving you was wrong and I no longer talked to you or played with you, but I secretly still wanted you. I feel shame about wanting you and excitement when I get to receive you. I am just so mixed up as to what I think and feel about you but I know that it is a love/hate relationship. When did it go so wrong?

Love,

Amy

Feelings: sadness, anticipation, fear

Dear Amy,

I know we used to play together and you used to love me. I miss you handling me, counting me, and paying attention to me. I feel like you abandoned me because you were told to not love me and not to want me and it was bad to like me. I am just a tool to be used to help you live the life you want. Won't you come out to play with me again?

Love,
Your Money

Feelings: sadness, hope

After you finish this coaching activity, read your letter out loud to a trusted friend, partner, advisor, or coach. By sharing the contents of your letters verbally, you will gather more insight into what is working and what is not working in your relationship with money. It is also a great way to practice talking about money with someone else.

Action & Accountability:

What action will you take as a result of this coaching activity?

Examples include continuing to write to money daily, weekly, or monthly or sharing this exercise with a significant person in your life.

_____

_____

_____

_____

_____

When will you take this action? In:

☐ 1 Day   ☐ 1 Week   ☐ 30 Days ☐ 60 Days   ☐ Not Taking Action Now

Who will be your accountability partner for this action step?

_____

Now that you started talking to your money, it is time to engage in a financial conversation with someone else.

Coaching Exercise #12:   Conduct a Financial Meeting

Purpose:

The goal of this coaching exercise is to practice and experience engaging in a healthy financial dialogue.

Getting Started:

This coaching exercise should take no more than 30 minutes to complete.

Pick a safe person to invite to your first financial meeting. This may be a trusted friend, wealth coach, romantic partner, business associate, or loved one. Select a time for the meeting that works for both parties. Make sure it is time that will be uninterrupted by work, children, or daily demands. Before the meeting, agree to a time limit. Make sure the time is set for 30 minutes or less. Any more time and the value of the coaching exercise may be lost.

Activity:

At the beginning of the meeting review the financial conversation guidelines together. Make sure each party understands the goal of the meeting is not to reach a consensus, but to really understand each other's perspective about money. This first meeting is setting the groundwork for future money communication so take your time.

Start the conversation by having Partner #1 answer the following question: What are you most proud of financially? By starting off on a positive note, you set the stage for sharing both the things you are satisfied with in your financial life as well as the areas you would like to improve on.

When Partner #1 is done answering the question completely, Partner #2 reflects back what he or she heard starting with the following words: "What I hear you saying is…" It is vital that Partner #2 sticks to the facts and when possible use your partner's exact words. Don't insert your judgment on what was said as this is not a time to express an opinion. Now switch roles and complete the exercise again.

After the conversation, both partners should answer the following questions in writing. Do this part separately at first and know that you will be sharing the information shortly.

1. What did I discover about my partner's beliefs and attitudes toward money?

   _____

   _____

   _____

   _____

   _____

2. How can I use these insights to engage in healthier financial conversations going forward?

   _____

   _____

   _____

   _____

   _____

3. What did I learn about myself in this conversation?

   _____

   _____

_____

_____

_____

4. How can I use this insight to help me have a healthier relationship with money and my partner?

_____

_____

_____

_____

_____

_____

_____

_____

Now share your responses with each other using the same active listening communication technique as before.

Action & Accountability:

What action will you take as a result of this coaching activity?

Examples include scheduling a date and time for a follow-up financial conversation or posting the financial conversation guidelines on the refrigerator as a visual reminder of the ground rules.

_____

_____

_____

_____

_____

When will you take this action? In:

☐ 1 Day ☐ 1 Week ☐ 30 Days ☐ 60 Days ☐ Not Taking Action Now

Who will be your accountability partner for this action step?

_____

Congratulations on taking the brave step to talk to someone about money! With time these money dialogues get easier so keep at it. Now that you have practice holding a financial meeting, it is time to start interviewing candidates for your financial dream team.

Chapter 9:   Your Financial Dream Team

A financial dream team is a group of professionals with a diverse set of skills that can assist you in determining and reaching your financial goals and objectives. There is so much to know in the world of finance that having a group of experts in your corner goes a long way to staying on top of the many aspects of your financial life.

How do you determine who should be on your team? Start by learning about different types of financial players and the special skill set each brings to the table. Below is a list of key financial services professionals and a brief definition of each one's role:

Accountant: A person trained to maintain, audit, and inspect financial records for individual or business entities. Often this person's role involves producing financial reports and tax return filing. A common credential in this field is the CPA, Certified Public Accountant.

Banker: An individual who works at a bank or financial institution such as a credit union is considered a banker. Retail bankers, the ones you typically see working in bank branches, work with individuals and families to provide products and services such as home mortgages, equity loans, and deposit accounts.

Commercial bankers work with businesses and corporations to provide products and services aimed at helping the business meet cash flow demands and fund commercial building and expansion.

Business Attorney: If you own a business, you will need a good business attorney on your team. These lawyers set up partnerships or corporations, check for compliance to regulations, obtain trademarks, prepare buy-sell contracts, and in general, counsel you on the legal part of your enterprise.

Estate Planning Attorney: An attorney who works with you and your family to create the appropriate legal documents to protect your wealth and assets is an estate planning attorney. They also help you communicate your wishes in the event of your death or a significant physical or mental disability. A good estate attorney conducts family meetings (often in conjunction with a wealth coach) to assist the family in communicating values, intentions, and the grantor's desired legacy. Upon death, they work with the beneficiaries to see the estate plan is followed.

Financial Planner: According to the Financial Planning Association, a financial planner is a professional trained to assist individuals in developing strategies to manage financial affairs so they can build wealth, enjoy life, and achieve financial security. The most commonly known credential in the field is the CFP, Certified Financial Planner.

Financial Therapist: According to the Financial Therapy Association which was formed in 2010, a financial therapist is defined as financial planner, financial counselor, therapist, psychologists, or social worker who provides advice, counsel, and therapy to their clients. Financial therapy blends aspects of financial planning, financial counseling, marriage and family therapy, sociology, social work, and psychology. Some financial therapists prefer to be called Money or Wealth Coaches.

Investment Manager: An investment manager typically works for a large financial institution, such as a bank, life insurance, or trust company to manage its portfolio or to provide management directly to third party clients. The investment managers most people are familiar with are mutual fund managers.

Money Coach: The profession of money and wealth coaching is new and therefore, the title of money coach can be used by a variety of professionals who coach individuals and business owners regarding money and finance. Some money coaches focus solely on get rich quick ideas (be warned!) and others combine good financial advice with support and accountability.

Wealth Coach: A wealth coach takes a holistic view of an individual's financial and non-financial resources and works with the person to help them have a better relationship with money. High quality wealth coaching involves challenging and supporting the client to make concrete behavioral changes and serving as a teacher, mentor, and accountability partner. The term wealth coach is often used interchangeably with money coach.

Wealth Manager: A financial services professional who offers a combination of services including investments, tax planning, estate planning, and legal counsel. As you can see, a wealth manager is a very broad term in the field and the definition is still widely debated.

QuickBooks Consultant: QuickBooks is popular financial software that many individuals and small businesses use to track and report on financial matters. A Certified QuickBooks Consultant is trained by the software company. QuickBook

Consultants help you set up your accounting system, teach you how to use it, and/or provide on-going bookkeeping services.

Buyer beware!

With any type of consultant, you want to screen each one carefully.

Unfortunately, there are some people in the financial services field, like any other industry, who do not have your best interest in mind. They may be out to make a quick buck or to gain access to your sensitive financial information.

Your screening and hiring process should be vigorous. It also helps to start your recruitment efforts by asking trusted friends, family members, and business associates for high quality referrals.

Next, start interviewing candidates. Here is a list of 10 powerful questions to ask a potential team member during a preliminary screening interview:

1. What are your professional credentials and what type of experience and training do you have in your specialty area?

2. How long have you been working in this field and why did you enter the field to begin with?

3. Who is your ideal client and what makes this client so great to work with?

4. Tell me about your greatest client success and what you learned from it.

5. Tell me about your greatest client failure and what you learned from it.

6. What concrete benefits will I realize from working with you?

7. How do you prefer to communicate with your clients and are you willing to match my communication style?

8. Do you have a support staff and if so, how will they help in our work?

9. Why should I hire you over someone else with the same skill set?

10. What else should I know about you that would help in my decision-making process?

Selecting a team player is an important decision. Do your research. Find out if the person belongs to a professional organization like the Financial Planning Association or the National Association of Personal Financial Advisors and then check to see if they are in good standing with the organization. Ask for references and then do your homework and follow-up by calling them. Any reputable financial services professional, coach, or consultant should welcome this type of due diligence. If the professional shows signs of being upset or annoyed by your questions and research, move on. Reputable and easy to work with coaches, advisors, and consultants are client-centric and therefore, welcome this type of inquiry.

Now that you have a definition of each team member and know what screening questions to ask, how do you know which members to recruit? The next coaching exercise, Build Your Financial Dream Team, will teach you how to determine the right mix for your team.

Coaching Exercise #13:   Build Your Financial Dream Team

Purpose:

This coaching exercise assists you in building your financial dream team.

Getting Started:

This coaching exercise involves building a support network which takes time. However, you should be able to complete the initial steps in this process in about 30 minutes. You will need a blank piece of paper, a writing instrument, and online access.

Activity:

Start by writing down all the financial matters you are currently responsible for handling. If you tend to avoid financial tasks, make sure you include the items that you avoid on the list as well.   If you start to get overwhelmed, just write down the first 10 items that come to mind.

Here's a sample list from a client:

Pay bills	*Balance checkbook*	*Send invoices to my clients*
Go to the bank	*Maintain insurance*	*Deal with medical bills*
Pay kids allowance	*Retirement savings*	*House errands*
Taxes	*Refinance home*	*Payoff car loan*

Now review the list and determine what type of financial services professionals could assist you with each task. Write the name of the professional beside the task. An example would be next to "Send invoices to my clients" you would write "QuickBooks Consultant." This does not mean you are hiring a bookkeeper right now. It means that you have identified a potential need for this type of professional on your financial dream team.

Now refer to the list below, putting a check mark next to each category of provider you eventually would like on your team. Feel free to add a category in the space provided if you do not see it listed below.

__ Accountant

__ Banker

__ Business Attorney

__ Business Partner

__ Estate Attorney

__ Financial Planner

__ Financial Therapist

__ Spouse/Partner/Loved One

__ You!

__ Wealth Coach

__ Wealth Manager

__ QuickBooks Consultant

__ Other: _____

Now prioritize your current needs by selecting the top three team members you want to put in place in the next 3 to 6 months. Write down the name of these professionals below in the order of importance:

1. _____

2. _____

3. _____

Next use Google to search each category to find out who in your area provides these services. Remember that some coaches and consultants work primarily by telephone; therefore, geographic location is not a factor.

Now that you have identified your top priorities, ask your inner circle of friends, family, and business colleagues for high quality referrals.   Notice if the same professional's name keeps coming up as this may be indicative of good reputation and expertise in the field.

The last step to this coaching activity will take a few weeks to complete. Call and set up screening interviews with 2 to 3 candidates in each of your high priority categories. Focus on one team player at a time and pace yourself. It takes a fair amount of time and energy to complete the screening and hiring process for each team player. But investing this time upfront ensures that your financial dream team will be strong, and meet your financial needs now and for years to come.

Action & Accountability:
What action will you take as a result of this coaching activity?

Examples include setting up an interview with a potential team member or talking with my romantic or business partner about my need for a financial dream team in my personal or professional life.

_____

_____

_____

_____

_____

_____

_____

When will you take this action? In:

☐ 1 Day   ☐ 1 Week   ☐ 30 Days ☐ 60 Days   ☐ Not Taking Action Now

Who will be your accountability partner for this action step?

_____

Excellent! You have a blueprint for your team and may even have a few members in place. Keep at this task until you have the financial support and expertise you need and deserve.

Chapter 10:   Practice, Not Perfection

Changing your relationship with money takes times, patience, and support. In this workbook you have learned a variety of tools for gaining more insight into your money mindset. You have defined what wealth means to you and the steps needed to attain it in your life. You have identified your money scripts and learned from your financial history. You have mastered a simple technique called the Mind Over Money Method (MOMM) for shifting your money mindset and you have practiced receiving wealth. And you have strengthened your money communication skills.   Yes, you have learned a lot!

As with any behavioral change, altering your financial attitude and habits takes time. Remember the stages of change and how it is human to take two steps forward and one back. Remind yourself that this is okay. It is to be expected. The goal is not to be perfect around money, but to practice being more skilled, more insightful, and less emotionally triggered by it. Practice, not perfection is what I tell my coaching clients. It is what I tell myself when it comes to my own relationship with money and it is a mantra I encourage you to adopt as well.

When you slip back into an old financial pattern or find yourself not taking steps forward toward creating the wealthy life you deserve, it is time to take a time out. During this time out, you want to recognize the troubling behavior and spend some time identifying the thoughts, beliefs, and feelings that triggered the event. By doing so, you will be able to turn this experience into a learning opportunity. And the best way to learn is by making mistakes!

The Guilty Lawyer: Matt

Let me give you a quick example of how this works:

Matt is a self-employed lawyer who hired me as a wealth coach. His main goal was to master his money mindset and be able to charge his clients what he felt like he was worth. By the time he ended coaching, Matt had mastered negotiating fees with clients and felt extremely confident in his worth. That was until he met Martha.

Martha was an elderly lady who came to Matt for help in drafting her will. She was a beautiful and kind older woman in her 70s and Matt really liked her. When he went to quote her his fee he found himself giving her his old rate – the one he had worked so hard to raise! When Martha left his office, he immediately gave me a call.

I assured Matt that backsliding happens and this was a great opportunity to learn something about his relationship with money. I asked him to describe Martha and what it felt like to sit with her in his office. Matt described her in detail and ended with the statement, "She reminds me of my mother." The moment he spoke those words he realized why he undercut his normal fee. "I felt guilty charging someone so nice and so much like my mother. I wanted to take care of her."

This client experience was invaluable as Matt discovered that when lovely, older women his mom's age contracted him for legal services he had to be very careful not to reduce his fee automatically.   By making this "mistake" and not being perfect in his fee negotiation, Matt took his work around money one step further and to a deeper place.

It is important to embrace any type of relapse in your money coaching as a slip that will teach you invaluable lessons. Do not overreact to these mistakes, but treat them with the urgency they deserve. By noticing when you fall into old money habits sooner, you are more likely to learn and grow from each experience and not let this behavior become habit again.

The following is a coaching exercise to help you when you take a step back into old money habits. Read through it now and make a note to use it as needed going forward. Just like a quick phone call to your coach can help you turn things around, so can this coaching activity.

Coaching Exercise #14:   Instant Money Replay

Purpose:

This coaching exercise is used to help you examine the thoughts, beliefs, and feelings that contributed to slipping back into an old money habit or financial behavior. By taking a snapshot you can hit replay and figure out what you would like to do differently the next time this situation occurs.

Getting Started:

It will take approximately 10 minutes to complete this coaching activity.

Activity:

First identify the event or situation that you would like to replay. This is called the "triggering event." Then complete the following questions to the best of your ability.

Triggering Event:

_____

- What did I say?

_____

- What did I do?

_____

- What did I feel?

_____

- What did I think?

_____

- What was the result?

_____

- What would I like to do differently?

  _____

- How would this change my feelings?

  _____

- How would this change my thoughts?

  _____

- How would this change the outcome?

  _____

Instant Replay:

If you could do this event over, what would it look like? Write out the new scenario here.

_____
_____
_____
_____
_____
_____
_____
_____
_____
_____
_____
_____
_____
_____
_____
_____

Action & Accountability:

What action will you take as a result of this coaching activity?

Examples include writing down the key lesson from this coaching activity and posting it where you can see it daily or developing an affirmation or mantra based on your instant replay.

_____

_____

_____

_____

_____

When will you take this action? In:

☐ 1 Day ☐ 1 Week ☐ 30 Days ☐ 60 Days ☐ Not Taking Action Now

Who will be your accountability partner for this action step?

_____

By setting the goal of practicing new money scripts and financial habits instead of the goal of perfection, you will continue to learn more each day about your relationship with money and how you can bring more wealth into your life.

Now it is time for some final thoughts as you complete this workbook.

Final Thoughts

Congratulations! You have completed the *Creating Wealth from the Inside Out Workbook*. By reading each chapter and completing each coaching activity, you learned easy, practical tools and techniques for examining and changing your relationship with money. You uncovered your money scripts, explored your family money history, learned about your money mindset, and how to take small steps to change unhealthy financial habits. You also practiced engaging in financial conversations and receiving wealth in your life. Lastly, you began the process of assembling your financial dream team. Yes, you worked hard and your reward is a wealthier and richer life.

Living a financially conscious life requires a long-term commitment to consistently putting words into action. Over time, many of these lessons will be integrated into your money psyche and become second nature. Use this workbook as a reference to guide you in your path toward true wealth. Revisit the chapters and coaching activities as needed and use the Appendices as a resource section for continued learning.

I would love to know how this workbook impacted you personally, so feel free to email me at kbk@kbkwealthconnection.com and let me know. I welcome your feedback and your success stories as well as learning the areas of money and wealth psychology where you would like me to delve deeper.

Thank you for allowing me to be part of your journey towards a wealthier you. It truly is an honor and makes my life so much richer.

kbk
Kathleen Burns Kingsbury, LMHC, CPCC
KBK Wealth Connection

Appendix I: A Wealth of Resources

The following is a list of books, websites, and other resources on wealth psychology and money management.

Books:

Benson, April Lane, To Buy or Not to Buy: Why We Overshop and How to Stop, Trumpeter Books, 2008.

Benson, April Lane, Ed., I Shop Therefore I Am: Compulsive Buying & the Search for Self, Jason Aronson Inc., 2000.

Burns Kingsbury, Kathleen, Creating Wealth from the Inside Out Audio, KBK Wealth Connection, 2010.

Burns Kingsbury, Kathleen, Creating Wealth from the Inside Out Workbook, KBK Wealth Connection, 2010.

Chatsky, Jean, Make Money, Not Excuses: Wake Up, Take Charge, and Overcome Your Financial Fears Forever, Three Rivers Press, 2008.

Chatsky, Jean, The Difference: How Anyone Can Prosper in Even The Toughest Times, Three Rivers Press, 2010.

Godfrey, Joline and Hinrichs, Kit, Raising Financially Fit Kids, Ten Speed Press, 2003.

Kahler, Rick and Fox, Kathleen, Conscious Finance: Uncover Your Hidden Money Beliefs and Transform the Role of Money in Your Life, Business Books, 2005.

Klontz, Ted, Kahler, Rick, and Klontz, Brad, The Financial Wisdom of Ebenezer Scrooge: 5 Principles to Transform Your Relationship with Money, Health Communications, Inc., 2006.

Kessel, Brent, It is Not About the Money: Unlock Your Money Type to Achieve Spiritual and Financial Abundance, HarperOne, 2008.

Klontz, Brad and Klontz, Ted, Mind Over Money, Broadway Business, 2009.

Perle, Liz, Money a Memoir: Women, Emotions, and Cash, Picador, 2006.

Price, Deborah, <u>Money Magic: Unleashing Your True Potential for Prosperity and Fulfillment</u>, New World Library, 2003.

Stanny, Barbara, <u>Secrets of Six Figure Women: Surprising Strategies to Up Your Earnings and Change Your Life</u>, HarperBusiness, 2004.

Stanny, Barbara, <u>Prince Charming Isn't Coming: How Women Get Smart About Money</u>, Penguin, 2007.

Trejos, Nancy, <u>Hot Broke Messes: How to Have Your Latte and Drink It Too</u>, Business Plus, Hatchette Book Group, 2010.

<u>Online Resources</u>:

360FinancialLiteracy.com: Free web-based program sponsored by the nation's certified public accountants to help Americans understand their personal finances through every stage of life.

FeedThePig.org: A website dedicated to helping you save money in a fun and informative way. You can sign up for weekly e-mail saving tips to help you stay on track.

KBKWealthConnection.com/blog: Updated two times weekly, this blog focuses on the psychology of money and behavioral finance. Using videos, podcasts, and written entries, the reader learns tips, tools, and strategies for creating wealth from the inside out.

Mint.com: This is a free web-based financial management system that helps you manage, save, and grow your money. It is secure and communicates with your bank and other financial institutions to provide you a real-time look at your financial situation upon request.

NEFE.org: Provides informative and user-friendly articles, tools, and other resources to help Americans acquire the knowledge and skills necessary to take control of their financial destiny.

WIFE.org: Women's Institute for Financial Education has helped women achieve financial freedom since 1998. WIFE co-founders are Ginita Wall and Candace Bahr.

StoppingOverShopping.com: This website hosted by author and psychologist April Lane Benson offers articles, books, podcasts, and videos addressing compulsive buying and shopping.

Professional Organizations

The following non-profit organizations provide referrals and information to consumers as well as education and training to professionals on financial planning, life planning, and financial therapy.

Financial Therapy Association: financialtherapyassociation.org

This organization is dedicated to educating consumers about financial therapy, establishing practice guidelines for professionals in this relatively new field, and conducting research on topics related to financial therapy and wealth coaching.

Financial Planning Association: FPAnet.org

The Financial Planning Association is a leadership and advocacy organization connecting the financial planning community.

National Association of Planning Financial Advisors: napfa.org

The National Association of Personal Financial Advisors is the nation's leading organization of fee-only comprehensive financial planning professionals.

Appendix II: Wealth Coaching Exercises

Here is an index of each of the coaching exercises for easy reference:

Coaching Exercise #1:   A Wealthy You 7

Coaching Exercise #2:   Your Money Scripts 13

Coaching Exercise #3:   Turn Up the Volume 17

Coaching Exercise #4:   Your Family Money Messages 24

Coaching Exercise #5:   Your Money Personality 30

Coaching Exercise #6:   Your Self-Esteem 39

Coaching Exercise #7:   Your Mind Over Money 48

Coaching Exercise #8:   How You Change 60

Coaching Exercise #9:   Your Stage of Change 63

Coaching Exercise #10:   Practice Receiving 69

Coaching Exercise #11:   Talk to Your Money 75

Coaching Exercise #12:   Conduct a Financial Meeting 79

Coaching Exercise #13:   Build Your Financial Dream Team 88

Coaching Exercise #14:   Instant Money Replay 95

Acknowledgements

As with any writing project, the *Creating Wealth from the Inside Out Workbook* was a team effort. I want to thank of all you who have helped me along my personal and professional path and especially the following:

The members of my writing group, Susan Hammond and Stacey Shipman, for their honest feedback and continued encouragement to write from my heart.

A writer is only as good as her editor, so a special thanks to Grace Talusan who edited this workbook.

To Kelly Pelissier, owner of Sage Hill Design, for her creative contribution to this workbook and her patience with the writer during the design process.

Fran Goldstein for her support, spirit, and all the pep talks she gave me when I needed them the most.

Leanna Hamill for lending her expertise and feedback on this project every step of the way.

Wendy Hanson for challenging me to think big and turn my passion for helping others into meaningful actions.

All my clinical and coaching clients for teaching me over the past two decades all I know about human behavior and change.

For those in the financial therapy and wealth counseling world who believed in me, my audio program, and my ability to have an impact in this field – James Grubman, Ph.D, Ted Klontz, Ph.D., Rick Kahler, CFP and April Benson, Ph.D.

My mother for teaching me the value of writing and for being my first editor.

My dad for raising me to be a financially literate woman before it was fashionable.

My husband, Brian Kingsbury, whose faith in me cannot be described in words. Thank you for your quiet and consistent encouragement, love, and for making me laugh every day. You truly make me a wealthy woman.

About the Author

Kathleen Burns Kingsbury possesses a unique blend of practical business know-how, financial expertise, and emotional intelligence that makes her a valuable resource to financial services professionals and their clients. She is an internationally published author, certified professional coach with a Masters Degree in Psychology, and an adjunct professor at the McCallum Graduate School of Business at Bentley University.

Voted one of the top ten executive coaches in Boston in 2009 by Women's Business, Kathleen is committed to helping her clients and her audiences bravely look at their relationship with money and become more emotionally and financially conscious. Working as a behavioral change specialist during the past two decades, she has acquired qualifications, skills, and knowledge of human behavior that few money coaches have in today's media-driven marketplace. Using humor, storytelling, and real-life experiences, Kathleen motivates and inspires people to make lasting financial behavioral change.

Kathleen experienced her own financial transformation when her family lost a large sum to a dishonest contractor and was forced to consider what true wealth was all about. Kathleen turned this negative experience into an opportunity to learn and grow. Soon after, she founded KBK Wealth Connection, a company dedicated to helping others create wealth from the inside out.

A member of the National Speakers Association, Kathleen has served as the Treasurer of the Board of Directors for the New England Chapter and on the finance committee. She is also a professional member of the International Coach Federation and the Financial Planning Association.

When she is not working, Kathleen is outside enjoying nature. She is an avid alpine skier who lives for the next powder day. In the off-season, she sails, hikes, and mountain bikes, using many of these experiences as inspiration for her writing and speeches.

CPSIA information can be obtained at www.ICGtesting.com
Printed in the USA
BVOW02s1134300114

343371BV00010B/596/P